The Western Wind Mass

by

John Taverner

Edited by

Anthony G. Petti

INDEX

CHESTER MUSIC

The cover illustration,
which has been used by kind permission
of the Bodleian Library, Oxford (MS. Mus. Sch. e. 378, f. 4ᴿ),
is an ornamental initial E from John Taverner's Mass "Gloria Tibi Trinitas".
It is reputed to be a portrait of the composer.

PREFACE

1. Biographical notes. There is still comparatively little known about John Taverner's life, and some of the few items that have normally been retailed are now called into question, including the notion that he became a fanatical Protestant, repented of having written music for the Latin rite and ceased composing after 1530.[1] He was born in Lincolnshire around 1490, but there is no certain information about him until 1524, when he was a lay clerk in the Tattershall collegiate choir. Two years later he became the first instructor to the choristers of Cardinal College (later Christ Church), Oxford. He left in 1530, when the college fell on hard times in the aftermath of Cardinal Wolsey's downfall. Returning to Lincolnshire, he obtained the post of lay clerk in the choir of St. Botolph, in Boston, a church richly maintained by the influential Guild of St. Mary. He prospered in Boston, was admitted to the Corpus Christi Guild, of which he became a treasurer in 1541-3, and was selected as an alderman for the newly incorporated town in 1545. He died in October of the same year. Taverner's extant works are not abundant by the standards of William Byrd, but they include eight complete masses (excluding the Kyrie), three Magnificat settings, over twenty motets, English adaptations of his Latin music, a handful of secular songs, and a couple of instrumental pieces.

2. The Western Wind melody. John Taverner's *Western Wind* Mass is one of three extant Early Tudor masses bearing that title, the others being by Christopher Tye and John Shepherd.[2] They are so named because their *cantus firmus* derives from a setting of the love lyric, "Westron wynde when wylle thow blow", which is extant, complete with melody, in the tenor part-book, MS. Royal, App. 58, f.5 in the British Library.[3] The *cantus firmus* is usually considered to be a variation on this tenor melody,[4] or a modified form of a descant to it supposedly concocted by the teenage Henry VIII.[5] Neither theory is satisfactory. The *cantus firmus* is scarcely closer to the tenor melody than to many other songs of the Henrician period, and nowhere in the masses is the putative original recognisably stated. It is no more convincing as a descant, for apart from being appreciably longer than the tenor melody, it is harmonically too improbable even for a remarkably unskilled and aurally insensitive composer, royal or otherwise.

A more likely possibility is that the *cantus firmus* stems from a completely different melody for the lyric, perhaps belonging to a three-part setting similar to the melismatic compositions of the Fayrfax Book,[6] being a "courtly" contrast to the "popular" tune of the Royal MS. A love poem as poignant as "Westron wynde" could well have been set more than once, as sometimes happens with 16th century English lyrics.[7] Certainly, what appears unconvincing as a variation or a descant, is a beautiful symmetrical and well-integrated melody in its own right, delicately balanced and conveying the meaning of the words at least as effectively as the tenor tune, especially in its sense of yearning and wistfulness, with the expressive leap in the opening incovation and the shapely descending melismas for "blow" and "rain". A reconstruction is given here, with the possible textual repetition and conjectural sharpened F indicated.[8] The ornamented cadences often found in bars 11, 14 and 21 in the masses are omitted.[9]

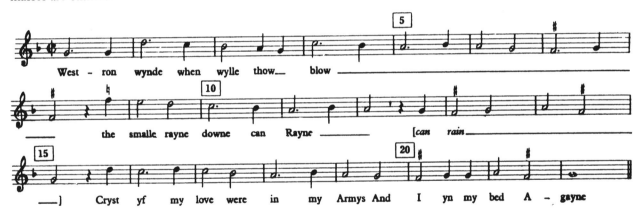

3. Sources and date of composition. The Taverner *Western Wind* mass survives in two 16th century sets of manuscript part-books, one in the British Library and the other in the Bodleian, Oxford. The British Library part-books, Additional MSS.17802-5, contain a large collection of Latin sacred music by English composers from the Henrician to the early Elizabethan period. They are usually known as the "Gyffard Part-Books", because they seem to have once belonged to a Phillip Gyffard,[10] and they are labelled Triplex (17803), Contratenor (17802), Medius (17804), and Bassus (17805). All three *Western Wind* masses are to be found in the part-books, being transcribed together in the order of seniority of the composers, and the authorship of each is clearly identified in every part in the main hand of the manuscript. The Triplex of the Taverner, for example, begins: "The Western Wynde mr taverner", and concludes: "finis Mr Taverner". The foliation for the Taverner is, Triplex and Medius, ff. 23v - 34; Contratenor, 25v. - 35v.; Bassus, 23 - 32v. The actual date of transcription of the whole manuscript is difficult to establish for either a *terminus quo* or *terminus quem*. It was obviously not compiled within a brief span of time, and the most liberal limits so far proposed, from the 1540s to the 1580s,[11] seem justified. The watermarks do not provide much help, since a time lag of at least thirty years has to be allowed for,[12] and much the same applies to the handwriting. There are two main scripts in the manuscript for the underlay and titling, presumably also representing different hands to judge from the penmanship. What seems to me to be the earlier hand and script (which I term Hand A) is a hybrid book hand of the early to mid-Tudor period, combining a *rotunda* Gothic text hand with a skilful amalgam of *Anglicana* and Secretary forms. The pen strokes are relatively even and made with a straight, somewhat blunted nib. The second hand and script (which I call Hand B) is in "bastard secretary", a hybrid book hand characteristic of the Elizabethan period, and examples of it are to be found in the copybooks of the 1580s and 1590s. In this case, the hybrid is a marriage of the *quadrata* text hand and Tudor secretary characteristic of the later 16th century. The nib is angled and there is much greater differentiation of ascenders and descenders.[13] The three *Western Wind* Masses are all written in Hand A for both music and underlay and seemingly copied out within a very short span of time, since the style is integral and continuous. My guess would place the transcription of all three masses between 1546[14] and 1560, with a preference for the later date. F.Ll. Harrison,[15] among others, has suggested that the part-books were transcribed in Mary's reign, possibly for Westminster Abbey. The suggestion is unlikely. They seem not to have been used for performance, since the large number of errors manifest in some parts of the manuscripts are uncorrected and, as stated above, sections of the manuscript are in a mature Elizabethan script.

Moving on to the state of the text, it is clear that the calligraphic skill exhibited in the *Western Wind* masses is not matched by musical accuracy, which is incredibly poor for the Taverner, though it becomes progressively better, with only about twenty mistakes for the Shepherd (but this is, after all, a shorter work, with fewer note clusters and notational variants). The scribe seems to have been conscientious and clearly made some attempt to check his transcription; as indicated by a few corrections made in his own hand while copying.[16] The fault seems to lie with the exemplum rather than the scribe. It is likely that he was working from three different manuscripts for the three masses, the one for the Taverner being particularly corrupt, as can be seen merely by glancing at the collation below. The corruptions are so extensive as to suggest that the exemplum itself was at least two stages removed from the composer's autograph, thereby allowing for the accumulation of the numerous errors in the work of an otherwise fairly trustworthy scribe.

The other source for the Taverner, the set of part-books in the Bodleian (MSS. Mus. e. 1-5), is far more dependable. It is commonly named after its undoubted compiler and original owner, John Sadler,[17] and, like the Gyffard set, comprises an anthology of Latin sacred music by Tudor composers, with the addition of a few motets by foreign composers and a couple of secular pieces. The part-books are in poor condition, mainly because the very corrosive iron-based ink has bitten through the rather thin paper and has eroded it in many places.[18]

Of the three *Western Wind* masses only the Taverner is included. It is the fortieth item in the collection (being one of four Taverner pieces), and is located as follows: e. 1(soprano), ff.68-72v.; e. 2(alto), 68-72v.; e. 3(tenor), 67v.-72; e. 5(bass), 62-66v.[19] As in the Gyffard, the authorship is consistently noted. The soprano part, for example, concludes with: "Quod m[r] John Taverner The Western Wynde ffinis". The date for the completed part-books is 1585, and this is obviously the *terminus quem* for the Taverner. However, although it is one of the last items in the book, the mass could have been transcribed by 1580. Indeed, the most recent suggestion is that it was copied out shortly after 1576, though I am not altogether convinced by the evidence propounded.[20] If one assumes a date around 1580, then this source for the Taverner is roughly twenty years later than the Gyffard transcription.

Sadler was somewhat less proficient in calligraphy than the Gyffard scribes, but he was nevertheless competent in the different forms of secretary, hybrid or otherwise, and in the traditional forms of *quadrata* (assuming that he is the sole copyist). The varied decorative features of the part-books also suggest that he had distinct leanings towards the medieval and the early baroque. His musicality is superior to that of the Gyffard Hand A, for his general accuracy seems backed by a consistent musical awareness, and his corrections sometimes seem to be those of a knowledgeable emender.[21] Most importantly, he was obviously working from an infinitely more dependable copy than the source for the Gyffard, especially in notational accuracy, amplitude of accidentals, and conviction of underlay. A rough assessment of obvious defects in notation (excluding accidentals) reveals that the Gyffard part-books have over forty fairly serious errors, including the omission of fourteen bars from the bass in the *Sanctus* (10-24). By contrast, the Sadler part-books have seven or eight consequential errors, mainly of a single note displaced one step on the stave. In underlay, the Sadler set is slightly more convincing and singable, with just three or four minor blemishes, one of which is debatable. Only in the time signatures is the Gyffard preferable, exhibiting a greater consistency and fullness. In addition to being generally superior, the Sadler set is entirely independent of the Gyffard. The two sources have no errors in common, they rarely coincide in the provision of accidentals, and the underlay is markedly different in many places.[22] Whatever the derivation of the exemplum for the Sadler, it is so reliable as to appear close in date to the composition of the mass, and is possibly only one remove from the autograph manuscript.

Concerning the actual date of composition there are several wide-ranging conjectures. Josephson opts for 1510-20 (and a London provenance), seeing the mass as Taverner's attempt to gain the favour of the young Henry VIII. He supports his claim on stylitic grounds by citing the uninterrupted stepwise figures encompassing a tenth (e.g., the bass of the *Sanctus*). But stylistic evidence has been invoked conversely to prove a late date. H.B. Collins asserts that "the prevalence of binary rhythm, as well as the masterly freedom of the counterpoint, point to the conclusion that it is one of the composer's latest works".[23] Others support a late date on the grounds of maturity of composition and the probability that Tye and Shepherd wrote their imitations shortly after as a tribute to the revered master, all three masses being placed in the early 1540s.[24] None of the evidence seems very convincing. However, the case for an early date is slightly strengthened by the likelihood that the secular melodies (or melody) were popular in the first two decades of the century, since Taverner might more plausibly have selected a song still in vogue than one thirty or forty years old. Nevertheless, Josephson's date seems a little early, and I would prefer a date closer to 1525.

4. Editorial method. Of the four editions published this century, two are truncated and rearranged versions for liturgical use; the other two are essentially collated versions of the two sources without a clear rationale for editorial choice.[25] In view of the undoubted reliability of the Bodleian copy and its vast superiority over the British Library version, I have followed it as faithfully as possible in every respect, including notation, accidentals, ligatures, coloration and underlay. Indeed, this is the first edition which attempts to follow the Bodleian underlay consistently. The British Library copy has been compared at every stage, and when, occasionally, it appears to have a preferred reading in notation, and, more commonly, when it indicates accidentals which accord with *musica ficta,* these have been incorporated and duly recorded in the textual notes. The F sharps of the *cantus firmus* have been preserved except when they appear to be unsingable harmonically, and have also been included from the British Library copy where possible. Most of them are undoubtedly in the hand of the transcriber in both sources, and also appear in the copies of the other two *Western Wind* masses. Unfortunately, there is no consistent application of the sharps in any of the three masses, nor any recognisable scheme of alteration. Some choirs may prefer to omit them altogether to preserve the modality, though to do so is a serious denial of the text.[26]

Since this edition is intended for performance as well as for study, bar lines have been introduced, note values have been halved in ₵ time and quartered in ⅔ passages, a dotted minim of the triple time equalling a minim of duple time. In *sesquialtera* (shown in the original by coloration with the sign 3 or 3 2),note values have been halved and grouped as triplets. I have not implemented the more fashionable practice of quartering the notation in duple time, since the resultant score would be more appropriate for string players than for choirs, the staves being heavily clustered with semiquavers and even demisemiquavers. The original key has been retained as being the most convenient and comfortable. If, however, the basses find difficulty with the low F, then the pitch can be raised a semitone or possibly a tone (see section 5 for range). Ligatures are indicated by slurs, coloration by ⌐ ¬, and underlay supplied by the Editor is in square brackets. Editorial accidentals are placed above the stave, being applied when consistency or *musica ficta* seem to demand them, albeit sparingly. 'Reminder' accidentals in the original are placed within the stave in round brackets. A keyboard reduction is also provided, with indications of tempo, proportions, dynamics and passages suitable for soloists. Plainsong intonations for the *Gloria* and the *Credo* have been supplied from the Sarum rite, there being none in the original. At the tempi suggested, the performance time is just under half an hour, each of the four sections lasting about seven minutes.

5. Clefs, signatures and ranges. The incipits' for both sources (except as noted in the collation) are:

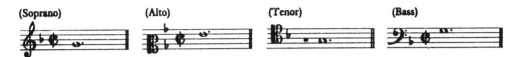

The Signature ₵ (most complete in the Gyffard) also occurs in the Gloria, 97, the beginning of the *Credo, Sanctus, Benedictus* and each of the three *Agnus Dei* sections (1, 66, 138). The signature $\frac{6}{2}$ (with note values double that of ₵ time) appears in the Gloria, 182, the *Credo,* 182, the *Agnus Dei,* 41 and 185. The Sadler part-books use as options to this form $\frac{6}{3}$ and $\frac{0}{32}$ (see Collation). Sesquialtera in duple time is represented by coloration, most usually with 3 2 inserted below at the beginning of the section in the Gyffard, and .3. in the Sadler. The ranges are as follows:

6. The Style. Since the Taverner setting has been the subject of a number of critical essays and notices, a long analysis of it is unnecessary here.[27] All three *Western Wind* masses are basically in duple time, but with several concluding sections in triple time. They are set for four voices, yet frequently reduce the texture by a large number of passages of duos and trios. The *Kyrie* is omitted (being usually performed in plainsong) and so are passages of the *Credo*. In Taverner's case, the cut extends from "Et in Spiritum" to "remissonem peccatorum". The Tye and Shepherd also make cuts from the *Gloria*. However, the most distinctive feature of the three masses is the use of a secular melody as a *cantus firmus*, a practice common enough on the Continent and popularised by Dufay and Josquin des Près, but virtually unknown in England until Taverner adopted it. The melody is set in the Dorian mode in all three, being transposed up a fourth in the Taverner and Shepherd, and is basically undisguised throughout and mainly without augmentation, though occasionally ornamented. Taverner is the most ambitious in his use of it, stating it thirty-six times and causing it to migrate to all but the alto line. Tye, by contrast, confines it to the very line from which Taverner excluded it; Shepherd keeps it mainly in the soprano.

One of the most noteworthy features of the Taverner is its fine sense of mathematical proportion. The four major liturgical divisions of the mass – the *Gloria, Credo, Sanctus/Benedictus* and the *Agnus Dei* (with the usual three sections) – are virtually equal in length, as revealed by the bar count and duration in performance.[28] More significantly, the thirty-six statements of the melody are equally distributed in sets of nine, so that each movement of the mass, presumably in deference to the Trinity, has a *cantus firmus* based on the square root of 9. But, as in Bach, proportions are not there *per se*. Although it is probably anachronistic to speak in terms of word-painting, the melody actually seems to vary in accordance with the mood of the text. It is sprightly in the opening expressions of praise in the *Gloria*, strongly affirmative in many of the expressions of faith in the *Credo*, expansively sonorous in the warm devotion of the *Sanctus*, quietly reflective in the *Benedictus* (as might be expected in the music closest to the Consecration), and gently supplicatory in the *Agnus Dei*. Taverner does not achieve these different effects by marked alterations of the melody or by modulation. Neither does he employ formal fugue. Indeed, most of the mass is homophonic and homorhythmic. The main stylistic means of variety and flexibility lies in judicious progression from the monosyllabic to the melismatic (without word repetition), the placement of the *cantus firmus* in a given part, the judicious combining of two and three voices, and the actual character of the variations or *obligati* that accompany a given melodic statement. Consider, for instance, the poignancy of the ATB combination for "Crucifixus" (*Credo*, 111 ff.), and how soulful the melody sounds in the bass, especially by contrast with its lightness in the soprano of the preceding trio for "Et incarnatus". It should be noted too, that Taverner maintains a rhythmic vitality throughout. For example, he closes the first two movements and the *Agnus Dei* with quick triple time codas, adding, for good measure, a flurry of triumphant Amens in the Credo; but, noticably, he does not pursue the obvious by ending the *Sanctus* the same way, as Tye and Shepherd do. He is also sensible of the fact that the last movement might well need the most variety: hence the extended passages of exquisitely lyrical triplets against duple time (*Agnus*, 23ff., tenor; 85ff. in the soprano and alto, taken up by the bass in a *Greensleeves* lilt, 107 ff.).

Virtually every device that Taverner uses is more than a characteristic of him or of the period: it is a subtle integral part of a beautiful whole. This applies, for example, to the medieval feature of progressing from the supertonic to the tonic at a cadence (*Agnus*, 183-4). The same is true of the other "archaic features of frequent huge spans of melismas and some hollow scoring for high and low voices".[29] The melismas of the *Sanctus* and *Agnus Dei* convey their meaning meditatively and emotively, in contrast to the more monosyllabic *Gloria* and *Credo*. It is also difficult to divine how the moving duet between the soprano and the bass in the plea for mercy in the *Gloria* (98ff.) could be improved by a different vocal combination—all the more so when it is viewed in the context of the other ensembles of the *Gloria*. But the mass needs no defence, and nearly all critics have been unstinting in their admiration of it. Of the most recent appraisals, only Josephson's contains reservations, mainly on the grounds of the apparent inflexability and dominance of the melody.[30] I hope some of my comments on the use of the *cantus firmus* will help to allay this worry. Further, it is salutary to remember that a Tudor mass was not a concert hall item or the uninterrupted side of a gramophone record or cassette, but a part of a much larger act of celebration and devotion. The breathing spaces which a liturgical performance affords, to say nothing of the total significance and setting, readily cause critical objections to evaporate or lapse into irrelevance. Whatever the circumstances of performance, the Taverner *Western Wind* mass can be counted an inspired offspring of the melody that gave it birth.

Notes

1 See further the *New Grove Dictionary of Music*, 1980, vol. 18, 598 ff., from which the present account is derived. The fullest treatment of the composer is by David S. Josephson, *John Taverner, Tudor Composer*, Ann Arbor, 1979

2 All three masses are published by J. & W. Chester/Edition Wilhelm Hansen London Ltd.

3 For a facsimile and transcription see N. Davison's edition of Tye, *Western Wind Mass*, J. & W. Chester, 1970, and A.G. Petti, *English Literary Hands from Chaucer to Dryden*, Arnold, 1977, 58-9, which also discusses characteristics of the hand.

4 e.g., P. Brett's note to his edition of Taverner, *Western Wind Mass*, Stainer and Bell, 1962. The *New Grove* (vol. 20, 375) describes it as a version of the same tune. Josephson, *op. cit.*, 43, believes it to be "a conscious and shrewd reworking of the original" by Taverner himself.

5 N. Davison "The *Western Wind* Masses", *Musical Quarterly*, 1971, 431 ff.

6 British Library, Add. MSS. 5456, edited by J. Stevens in *Musica Britannica*, vol. 36, 1975. The notion of two separate tunes seems to have been first propounded by H.E. Wooldridge in *Old English Popular Music by William Chappell*, 1, 1893, 37-8, who provides transcriptions of both (inaccurately described as "versions" in *New Grove*, loc. cit., bibliography, 376). I was unaware of the Wooldridge reference when I first proposed two separate tunes in the Preface to my edition of the Shepherd *Western Wind* Mass, 1976.

7 In the Fayrfax MS., for example, which is fairly close in date to MS. Royal App. 58, there are two separate settings of *Wofully araid*, one by Cornish and the other by Browne (*Musica Britannica*, vol. 36, nos. 53 and 55). It is also possible that there are two separate lyrics having the same title. In this respect it should be noted that there are two sets of Henrician lyrics and tunes for "I have been a foster", though the lines have something in common for the first ten measures (cf. *Musica Britannica*, vol. 18, 1962, no. 62, and *Musica Britannica*, vol. 36, 1975, no. 1). Also to be remembered is that there were two totally unrelated tunes called *L'homme armé*.

8 The sharps are indicated here because they occur (albeit inconsistently) in all three masses. It is likely that the secular melody had no sharpened leading notes, but that these were added when the melody was adapted for the masses. Plainsong was also often subjected to this treatment when incorporated in polyphony (cf. *Tudor Church Music*, vol. 1, *John Taverner*, 1923, xli). Later in the century, the raised leading note can be found in the actual plainsong service books, as in Guidetti's *Directorium Chori*.

9 The ornamented version is given in my Preface to the Shepherd *Western Wind* mass. My underlay is highly conjectural; Wooldridge, though he did not attempt one, suggested (*op. cit.*) that the last two lines of the poem were repeated. This would involve beginning the second line in bar 5, the third in bar 8, and the fourth in bar 12. My own preference derives from an interpretation of the poem which involves (as implied by the bar and *fermata* of the Royal MS. setting) a clear separation of "blow" from the "rain". My paper on the subject is to appear shortly.

10 See further, R.W. Bray, "British Museum ADD. MSS. 17802-5 (the Gyffard Part-Books): an Index and Commentary", *R.M.A. Research Chronicle*, no. 7, 1967, 31-50. Though useful, the article is understandably tentative in its conclusions, and makes no reference to palaeographical evidence apart from watermarks.

11 Bray, *op. cit.*, especially 50.

12 Cf. Bray, *op. cit.*, 49 etc.

13 For description of the scripts referred to *vid*. Petti, *English Literary Hands from Chaucer to Dryden*, esp. 13-17.

14 Tye is termed "Doctor" throughout the part-books. He received his D. Mus. in 1545.

15 *Music in Medieval Britain*, 1958, 289. See also, K.R. Long, *The Music of the English Church*, 1971, 65.

16 e.g., the corrections on the second page of the Triplex, top stave, in which a dotted minim and crotchet are changed to a semibreve and minim.

17 See further, David G. Mateer, "John Sadler and Oxford Bodleian MSS Mus. e. 1-5", *Music and Letters*, 1979, 281-95. Sadler's signature and monogram are liberally interspersed throughout the part-books.

18 I am especially indebted to R.W. Hunt the then Keeper of Manuscripts at the Bodleian Library for allowing me to consult the original manuscript in the early seventies. The Bodleian also has a microfilm copy of the manuscript, though it is very difficult to read, the notation from the underside of a leaf frequently almost coalescing with that on the top.

19 The part-books are unlabelled, so I have used modern terms in this description and in the collation. The Gyffard labels are noted in this section and in the table of abbreviations for the collation.

20 Mateer, *op. cit.*, 287.

21 Space does not permit expansion of this important topic. Clearly, to reach tenable conclusions on the nature of the text far more searching analytical methods must be employed than have so far been used on either the Gyffard or the Sadler. It should be noted that Sadler was also a composer, and one of his motets concludes the part-books.

22 I have encountered only one place where the sources share what appears to be an unsingable accidental, the C sharp in the Alto of the *Credo*, 26, i. It is doubtful whether this constitutes a common error. The case is further complicated because the C sharp is linked to a possible F sharp in the soprano at that point in the Bodleian copy.

23 See further, Josephson, *op. cit.*, 41-4, 140-2; H.B. Collins, preface to his edition of the *Western Wynde*, 1924. It should be remembered that over a hundred years separate the first and last *L'homme armé* masses.

24 Cf. the *New Grove* article on Taverner, 601; and N. Sandon's preface to his edition of Shepherd's masses (*Early English Music*, xviii, p. x).

25 These editions are respectively by H.B. Collins (1924), Dom Anselm Hughes (1924), *Tudor Church Music*, vol. 1 (1923) and P. Brett (1962).

26 Collins, *op. cit.*, repented of including so many F sharps. *T.C.M.* includes most of them; so does Brett, though in the recording by King's College Cambridge based on his edition (Argo ZRG 5316) they are all omitted. By contrast, the most recent recording, by New College Oxford (CRD 1072), observes as many as possible. Davison includes most of the sharps in his edition of the Tye, but again, the King's College recording (Argo ZRG 740) omits them, and so does the most recent edition, by P. Doe (*EECM, 1980*). In the case of the Shepherd, the Sandon edition (*op. cit.*) omits them, mine includes them, and so does the recent recording by St. John's College, Cambridge. See also note 8.

27 Most of these are listed in the *New Grove* bibliography to the Taverner article. Among the most useful are the works of Harrison and Davison listed in notes 5 and 15, the Josephson book (note 1) and the article by T. Messenger, "Texture and form in Taverner's 'Western Wind Mass'", *Journal of the American Musicological Society*, xxii, 1969, 167ff.

28 In this edition the numbers of bars are 205, 205, 203, and 208. In Brett's edition they are 103, 102, 102, 104. H. Benham (*Latin Church Music in England, 1460-1575*, 1975, 226-7), uses a little sleight of hand to reduce these numbers to 97 for the *Sanctus* and exactly 100 for each of the others.

29 The *New Grove* article on Taverner. The quotation is a general comment on his work.

30 *op. cit.*, 141-2.

THE WESTERN WIND MASS

Gloria

Edited by
ANTHONY G. PETTI

John Taverner
(c.1490-1545)

2

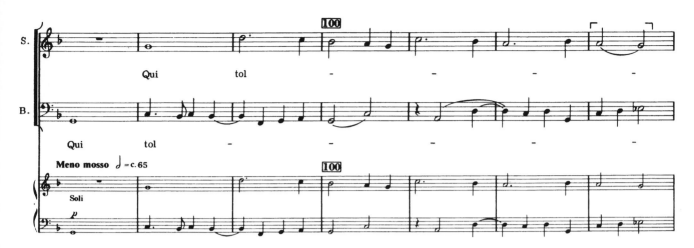

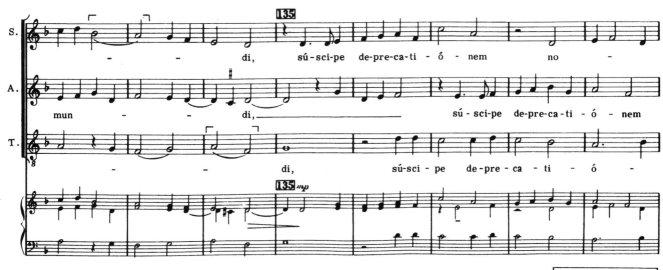

185
S.
A.
T.
B.
Cum San - cto Spí - ri - tu in
Cum San - cto Spí - ri - tu, Spí - ri -
Cum San - cto - - - - cto Spí - ri - -
Cum San - - cto Spí - ri - tu
Vivace ♩=c.180 (♩.=♩)
f
190
195
gló - ri - a De - i Pa - tris. A -
- tu in gló - ri - a De - i Pa -
- tu in gló - ri - a De - i Pa - -
in gló - ri - a De - i Pa - - tris. A -
200
205
- - - - - - men.
- tris. A - - - - men.
- tris. A - - - - men.
- - - - - - men.
sempre f
f
poco rall.

Credo

Sanctus

Benedictus

Agnus Dei

39

Collation and textual notes. Since this edition is based on the Bodleian part-books, the collation mainly records the British Library variants, except where the Bodleian reading seems wrong. The ligatures and coloration of the British Library copies have not been noted, neither has the underlay, unless it contains a preferred reading. Occurrence of 'reminder' B♭ in Bass is not normally recorded. Note and rest values are given as in the original.

Table of abbreviations

O	Bodleian MSS., Mus. Sch. e. 1-5	em.	emended editor
L	British Library, Add. MSS. 17802-5	nat.	natural
S	Soprano (Triplex)	om.	omitted
A	Alto (Contratenor)	supp.	supplied from
T	Tenor (Medius)	c	crotchet
B	Bass (Bassus)	m	minum
TCM	Tudor Church Music Edition	sb	semibreve
abs.	absent from	b	breve
		l	longa

Gloria

Prelims. **B**, flat om. throughout Mass, L; 1 **T**, sig. om., L; 7 i **S**, sharp om., L; 10-11 **T**, FEAG for AGCB♭, L; 11 ii **B**, nat. abs. L; 12 iv **B**, flat om., L; 14 ii **A**, flat supp. L; 15 i **A**, nat. abs. L; 16 iii-iv **S**, sb for two ms, L; 21 i **A**, dotted sb for sb,0, em. from L; 21 iii-iv **T**, sb for two ms, L; 21 iii-iv **B**, two ms for sb and flat abs. L; 23 i **B**, nat. om L; 37 i **S**, sharp om.0, supp. L (misrecorded TCM); 43 i-iii **S**, dotted sb, L (misrecorded TCM);65 iii-66 iii **A**, "ge-ni-" set one note later, O, em. from L; 66 iii-iv **B**, two ms for sb L; 68 iii **A**, flat om. L; 69 iii **B**, flat om. L; 70 i **S**, sharp supp. L; 71-2 **T**, two bs for 1, L; 73 **S**, two ms and sb, L; 74 ii **B**, A in O, em. from L; 79 i **S**, sharp O, em. from L; 80 i **A**, m for sb, L; 80 iii **B**, superfluous sb on B♭, L; 81 iii **A**, flat abs. L; underlay "A-" one note early, O,em. from L; 89 iii **A**, A in L; 94 i **A**, nat. abs. L; 96 i **A**, nat. om. L; 97, sigs ₵ in **SB**, L, none in O; 104 i-iii **B**, dotted sb, L; 105 **B**, nat. before E abs. O, supp. L; 114 **B**, nat.before E in L; 115 iv **B**, m on D for c DE in L (misrecorded TCM); 142 iii **T**, sharp om. O, supp. L; 147 i-iii **S**, sb and m on C, L; 150 iv **B**, flat om. L; 151 **A**, two sbs for b, L; 153 i - 154 ii **T**, b and sb, L; 154 i **A**, sharp abs. L; 155 iii-iv **S**, sb in L; 155 iii **B**, flat om. L; 158 i **A**, flat om. L; 160 iii - 161 i **A**, dotted sb L; 161 iii **A**, nat. abs. L; 175 i **B**. nat. added L; 182 sigs. ₈ in all parts, L; **S**, ₃₂⁰, **AT** ₃⁰, **B**₃⁸ in O; 183 i-ii **B**, two sbs; L; 192 **A**, one (dotted) b rest om. L; 198 iii **T**, redundant sb G after rest in L; 200 iii - 201 i **T**, m D, dotted m C and c C in O, em. from L; 204 i **A**, nat. om. L.

Credo

Prelims., sigs. om. **STB** in O, T in L; 3 iii **B**, flat om. L; 5 iv **B**, nat. abs. L; 7 iii **S**, sharp in O, em. from L; 8 iii **B**, flat om. L; 10 ii **B**, C in L; 13 i-ii **T**, FE for AG in L; 14 iv **A**, two cs for m, L; 22 iv **S**, superfluous m G in L; 23 iv **S**, flat added; 26 i **S**, sharp in O, em. from L; 26 i **A**, sharp, O and L, em.; 29 i **S**, misrecorded TCM; 35 i **A**, A in L; 41 ii-iii **A**, sharp in O, em. from L; B for D in L; 46 iii **T**, A for G in L; 48 iii **B**. flat om. L; 54 ii **A**, two cs for m, L (pref. reading?); 54 iii **T**, flat om. O, em. from L; 58 i **A**, m for two cs, L; 62 i-iii **A**, sb m for m sb, L; 72 iii **A**, flat abs. L; 75 i-ii **B**, three ms. L; 80 i **A**, nat. om. L; 85 i **B**, "cae-" om. O; 87 iv **A**, nat. om. O, supp. L; 92 **B**, dotted sb and m om. L; 95 iii - 96 ii **B**, dotted m and c for dotted sb and m, L; 101 i **S**, sharp in L; 102 iii **S**, sharp abs. L; 103 ii **A**, flat abs. L; 104 iii-iv **S**, sb for rest and m, L; 108 iii **B**, flat om. L; 110 iii **S**, sharp abs. L; 110 ii **B**, misrecorded TCM (flat neither in O nor L); 114 i **B**, two ms for sb, L; 118 i-ii **A**, F for G, L (pref. reading?); 124 iii-iv **S**, nat. abs. L; 130 i **A**, sharp om. L; 131 iii **T**, flat om. O, supp. L; 134 **T**, nat. om. L; 144 iii **B**, B♭ for C, L; 147 iii **A**, flat om. L; 148 ii **A**, nat., L; 149 i **A**, nat. om. O, supp. L; 150 ii **B**, F for G in O, em. from L; 153 ii **A**, nat. om. O, supp. L; 154 iii **A**, flat om. O, em. from L; 156 **B**, two As for Fs, L; 158-159 **B**, two bars om. L; 161 iv **T**, C for D in L; 167 iii **A**, flat om. L; 169 iii **T**, flat om. L; 170 iii **T**, flat om. L; 171 i-iii **T**, sb and rest, O, em. from L; 172 i **A**, flat om. L;

172 iii **T**, flat om. L; 175 iv **A**, two ms for two cs, L; 175 i **T**, flat abs. L; 178 iii **A**, nat. abs. L; 182 sigs., all parts, ₃⁸, L; **SB**₃⁰**AT**₃⁸, O; 182 i **T**, flat, L; 190 ii-iii **T**, D for E, O, em. from L; 194 iii **S**, b for sb, L; 195-6 **S**, two bars om. L; 204 **B**, flat abs. L.

Sanctus

Prelims., no key sigs. in O; 7 iv **A**, flat before B♭ abs. L; 9 i **A**, F for G in L; 9 i **T**, D for C in L; 10 i **T**, m rest missing L; 10-24 **B**, om. L; 23 **S**, sb and sb rest, L; 24 iii **T**, flat abs. O, supp. L; 35 i-iii **S**, dotted sb, O, em. from L; 37 iii **S**, sharp abs. L; 41 iii - 42 ii **T**, b for dotted sb m, L; 54 iii **A**, flat abs. L; 60 iii **S**, sharp abs. L; 71 ii-iii **S**, sb, L; 72 ii **S**, superfluous? "-ni", O; 74 i **S**, sb om. L; 76 i **S**, flat om. L; 83 iii **S**, nat. om. L; 84 **S**, nat., L; 96 i-iii **B**, dotted sb, L; 106 iii **B**, sharp, L; 111 iii **A**, D for C, L; 119 i **T**, E for F, L; 123 i **A** misrecorded TCM; 123 iii **A**, nat abs. O, supp. L; 123 i **B**, flat abs. O, supp. L; 124 ii-iv **A**, dotted sb, L (pref. reading?); 129 i **S**, sharp, O (poss. deleted) em. from L; 130 iii **S**, sharp abs. L.

Benedictus

Prelims., sigs. om. O, and **SA** in L; 16 ii **B**, flat om. L; iv **B**, redundant sb and m rest, L; 17 i-iii **T**, sb and m rest O, em. from L; 17 ii **B**, nat. before E abs. O, supp. L; 20 ii **B**, D for C in L; 21 iv **B**, nat. abs. L; 23 i **B**, nat. abs. L; 37 i **S**, sharp abs. L; 44 ii **S**, sb for m, L; 45 iv **B**, nat. in L; 46 ii **B**, nat. abs. L; 62 i **S**, sb for m., L; 67 ii **A**, G for F, L; 69 iv **S**, nat. om. L; 70 **S**, nat. om. L.

Agnus Dei

Prelims., sigs. om. **SAB** in O; om. **A** in L; 13 i **B**, sharp abs. L; 14 iii **B**, sharp abs. O, supp. L; 22 i **S**, sharp L; 25 i-iii **S**, dotted sb, L; 32 i-ii **B**, three black ms for black m sb, L; 41, sigs. ₃⁸ all parts L, and **SAT** O; **B**₃⁸ bar 42, O; 45 ii **A**, G for F, L; 47 ii **A**, D for C in L; 50-51 **B**, (black notation) b sb sb sb sb for sb b b sb L; 51 iii **T**, sb rest om. L; 54 i **S**, sharp abs. L; 56 i **A**, nat. om. O, supp. L; 58 ii **B**, G for F in L; 62 i **S**, sharp in O, em. from L; 63 ii **S**, sharp in O, em from L; 64 i **B**, nat. om. L; 66 sigs. **TB** in L, none in O; 73 i-ii **A**, three black ms., L; 88 ii-iii **A**, two black ms for black sb, L; 89 iii **A**, nat abs. L; 90 iii **S** - 91 iv **S**, dotted b for b and sb rest, L; 90 i **A**, black m on D om. L; 90 ii **A**, nat. om. O, supp. L; 106 ii **B**, '-ta' om. O, supp. L; 108 i **B**, flat abs. L; 109 i-ii **B**, three black ms, L; 110 i-ii **B**, three black ms, L; 111 iv **B**, flat before B, L; 131 i **A**, m for sb, L; 131 i **T**, m rest for m, L (pref?); 138, sigs. om. O, all parts, **SA** in L; 139 **T**, black b and two cs, L; 140 iii - 141 ii **S**, dotted sb and two cs (no coloration) L; 140 i **A**, sb on F, L; 150 iii **A**, nat., L; 153 i **A**, nat. om. L; 157 iii **S**, G for A in O, em. from L; 158 iii-iv **B**, m rest and m. L; 160 i **S**, sharp om. O, supp. L; 161 i **A**, flat abs. L; 177 ii **A**, flat abs. L; 184 iii **A**, nat. om. L; 185 sigs. ₃⁸ **SAB**, ₃⁰ **T** in O, **SATB** ₃⁸ in L; 191 i **S**, sharp abs. O, supp. L; 194 ii **B**, F for G in L; 198 **A**, DB for ED in L; 199 i **A**, nat. abs. L; 199 iii **A**, flat in L; 206 ii **T**, sb for b, L; 207 i **B**, nat. om. L.

The Chester Books of Madrigals
Edited by Anthony G. Petti

The Chester Books of Madrigals offer an exciting collection of secular European madrigals, partsongs and rounds from the 16th and early 17th centuries, newly edited from early sources by Anthony G. Petti, who contributes copious historical notes to each volume.

The majority of the settings are for SATB, and simplified keyboard reductions with suggested tempi and dynamics are provided as a rehearsal aid or as a basis for a continuo part where appropriate. Texts are in the original languages, English, French, German, Italian and Spanish, with modernised spelling and punctuation. In the case of the non-English texts translations are provided at the head of each piece.

An important feature of this anthology is the arrangement by subjects. which, it is hoped, should be of great assistance in programme planning. Indispensable popular works are interspersed with relatively unfamiliar but attractive and singable pieces.

チェスター社マドリガル楽譜シリーズ

このシリーズは、16世紀から17世紀初頭のヨーロッパのマドリガルと合唱曲を、目的別に集めたユニークなアルバムです。各巻はテーマ別に分けられ、第一巻は**動物**、第二巻は**愛と結婚**のシリーズになっています。各巻の解説にあるようにコンサートのプログラム作成にも便利です。

編成は混声四部合唱ですが、混声三部又は五部のものも若干含まれ、六部の曲もあります。

この曲集に入っているマドリガルは、最も有名でポピュラーなもの、魅力的で歌いやすいが余り知られていないもの等です。歌詞は、曲によってオリジナルの英語、イタリア語、フランス語、ドイツ語、及びスペイン語がついています。

チェスター社の**モテット楽譜シリーズ**と同様、この**マドリガル楽譜シリーズ**は演奏用、又は研究用に適するものとして作成されています。又、最も権威ある原典を資料にしていることは、音楽専門家にとって大変参考になります。

1. The Animal Kingdom
2. Love and Marriage
3. Desirable Women
4. The Seasons

In preparation

5. Singing and Dancing
6. Smoking and Drinking

CHESTER MUSIC